MW00827774

THE Rocks COME WITH THE Farm

How to Prepare for, Plow Through, and Profit from Tough Times

JONAH MITCHELL

dustjacket

Dust Jacket Press
P.O. Box 721243
Oklahoma City, OK 73172
www.dustjacket.com

Dust Jacket logos are registered trademarks of Dust Jacket Press, Inc.

Cover & Interior Design: D.E. West / ZAQ Designs - Dust Jacket Creative Services

Printed in the United States of America

www.dustjacket.com

DEDICATION

In the Great Halls of the History of Papas and Grand-daughters, there have been many who have loved their granddaughters with love that was extraordinarily sweet and life-fulfilling, but none more than this Papa. I dedicate this book to my precious granddaughters, Caitlin Jean Mitchell and Aubrey Elizabeth Mitchell.

TABLE OF CONTENTS

INTRODUCTION

*O*n *Valentine's Day, Mimi rushed me to the ER and we soon learned I was in the middle of a heart attack. I surprised even myself by being a perfect patient—calm, compliant, not overly anxious. Of course, I was under the care of Dr. James Blake, an exceptionally talented emergency medicine doctor.*

All the time, I was thinking about what I had recently heard on Ted Talk radio by a palliative care doctor who said that in emergency, near-death situations, he found people are generally most concerned about three things:

Forgiveness. (Giving or receiving.)

Has my life had meaning? (Tell me I've been a good person.)

How will I be remembered? (Am I leaving a legacy?)

Your Papa had no problem with these three. I trusted my Savior that my many sins were forgiven. I have always believed Mimi when she says I'm a "good man." I knew Jason, your dad, would carry the torch.

Only once did I stop the entire process of tests, wires, ambulances, prescription drugs, reports, and more tests. I insisted that I was not to be sedated until I had spoken to you girls. At that moment, I promised Mimi I would write you a letter of my love and for your guidance.

Here it is.

Love, Papa

PROLOGUE

I want my precious granddaughters to know who I am. So, when they go mining for the ingredients that make them who they are, they will be able to stir up the rich flavors of our mountain heritage, those bold genuine characters we call family and friends, and tap into the unique grit and gifts that I was privileged to receive and now pass on to them.

If you take away the badges, titles, degrees, awards, and daily expectations . . . *who am I?*

I am the littlest boy running down those nine wide porch steps of our unpainted, tin roof house, two at a time. We had just completed the chores of filling the kindling box, toting the fresh milk over from pap and ma's, and hanging the quilts on the house porch railing. We were off to the uncovered front porch of my dad's general store. I just had to beat June Bug, Caroline, and Reva Mae to the best place to sit in the shade and be the first to finish stringing our pop lid snake toy. Mitchell's General Store was half-covered with rusting metal signs advertising RC Cola, Nehi "pop," marshmallow Moon Pies, and Robin Hood Flour. A Sunbeam Bread ad was stenciled across the screen door. That porch was the general daily meeting place for all concerns, large and small, up and down the road between Roxana and Kingdom Come. Yes, there is a Kingdom Come. My dad attended school there. Other settlements nearby were Blackey, Rockhouse, Leatherwood, Big and Little Cowan, Viper, Caney Creek, Troublesome, Hot Spot, and Hell-fer-sartin.

But the center of my universe was that porch.

Almost everything important happened or was discussed on that porch in good weather, or inside around the pot-bellied stove on stormy or cold days.

The only exception was the visit of President Lyndon B. Johnson during his war on poverty TV tour. He visited my Uncle Hiram's store instead of Dad's, but that was years later and two miles away in Roxana anyway.

The first customers that memorable morning at Dad's store were Manious and Tilldy Isom, and nobody seemed to recall how long they had been gone from the mountains.

"Who are you?" Manious asked.

"I'm the littlest Joner, JC."

"Are you Pap Mitchell's young'n?" Manious replied.

"No, I'm Chester's second boy."

"You talk'n about old Joner Mitchell's middle boy, Check?" Manious exclaimed.

"Yes sir, that's who I am. Check's boy!"

Old Jonah Mitchell, the patriarch, fathered ten or so children at the head of Muddy Branch. His amalgamated compound included two bunkhouses, a log cabin, and a separate detached log kitchen with a dirt floor and a gigantic rock fireplace, complete with double-hung swinging irons for the cooking pots.

My dad married early and tried deep-shaft coal mining, but never seeing daylight Monday through Saturday took its toll. He just had to breathe fresh mountain air. He and his fifteen-and-a-half-year-old bride settled down at the mouth of the branch, built a house next to Alma and Watson Whitaker's place, right on Highway 160, directly across the road from our two-room whitewashed schoolhouse, and of course opened his store.

That's where I come in.

One of thirteen children, born to Amanda Cornett Mitchell.

Three died in infancy.

Six were born in poverty.

Four more were born with her hard-working iron-boiler-maker second husband, Hubert Ray Edwards.

My early journey weaves a pattern through relative poverty and hardship, including double-bronchial pneumonia with burst eardrums, along with the good memories, such as sled riding in the deep snow, hog kill'n with cracklins, and lard making. I'll never forget those pie auction suppers. A couple of "orphanages" came along, which were actually children's homes, named Smootcreek and Buckhorn.

This is where you join in.

Enjoy *The Rocks Come With The Farm.*

SECTION I

How to Prepare for Tough Times

CHAPTER ONE

The Rocks Come with the Farm

"If we do not sometimes taste of adversity,
prosperity would not be so welcome."
—Anne Bradstreet

The sheets of snow and ice were flying; you could hear and see the bitter cold between the cracks of the clapboard two-story bunkhouse of Buckhorn Children's Home on Squabble Creek in the mountains of Eastern Kentucky. Boys on the second floor, upper and lower bunkbeds against the walls, a center aisle, coal-fired cast iron pot-bellied stove on the north end, and an out-of-tune upright piano on the other end.

We all huddled around the stove, first warming our frontsides and then our backsides. Everyone made a mad scramble to their beds, covering all but a breathing hole. We shivered, rubbed, tossed and turned to create some warmth. The lucky ones were wearing long johns.

Then it started . . . down by Chub's bed on the other end; the voices were low, but the harmony was sweet . . .

Froggy went a courtin' and he did ride . . .
uh-huh, uh-huh,
With a sword and a pistol by his side . . .
uh-huh, uh-huh,
He rode up to Miss Mousey's door . . .
uh-huh, uh-huh,
Where he had been many times before . . .
uh-huh, uh-huh . . .

We sang and laughed and forgot about everything else until we heard "lights out!" Every boy went to sleep dreaming of hot summer days, catching crawdads hiding beneath the shadows of those smooth, round Black Mountain rocks in Kings Creek's cool waters. Sleep came as a sweet release.

"June Bug! June Bug! June Bug! I'm cold. I'm really cold!" June Bug rolled off the top bunk, grabbed his weathered, woolen coat from the nail hook, put it on, and pulled one of his quilted blankets off his bed and covered that crying little boy, rubbing the blanket good and hard.

June Bug whispered, "We're going to get through this! Now, go to sleep." He crawled back under his only blanket, wrapped tight in his overcoat.

June Bug was my older brother, and I was that cold, little five-year-old boy. *A brother is born to help in the time of adversity* (Proverbs 17:17).

June Bug understood that we were deep into tough times. Guided by his heartfelt understanding, compassion, and sacrifice, he gave me the greatest gift possible, when it appeared he had nothing to give at all. A tattered old hand-stitched hand-me-down patchwork quilt blanket, yes, but the truth is, the gift was *love* for his freezing little brother, and with it, the greatest lesson ever taught.

As I write this, I am still filled with strong emotions and precious memories of June Bug's care and love.

Others long ago came to the same understanding; I had to, you have to:

"If we had no winter, the spring would not be so pleasant; if we did not sometimes taste of adversity, prosperity would not be so welcome."[1]

That great lesson taught to me by June Bug, I now give to you: *The Rocks Come with the Farm!*

It is certainly true around our Jessamine County farmhouse, filled with more love and laughter than any Papa or Mimi could ever have dreamed of. I'll never forget Aubrey's words one cool Thanksgiving evening as she laid her sleepy head on Mimi's lap, watching the fire in our big stone fireplace, and said, "This is paradise." I can still see my granddaughters as youngsters, crawling and climbing on our large pile of set-aside rock slabs.

The rocks here in Kentucky are karst topography porous limestone, just under the topsoil—layered, thick, centuries-old bedrock. In Arizona, there are red rocks; in Hawaii, lava rocks; blue stone in New York, and in South Dakota, solid granite. It's a Stone Mountain in Georgia, and what about Boulder, Colorado?

Our everyday lives are filled with and surrounded by rocks, rock ledges, palisades, deep mountain roadway cuts, and natural rock bridges. Of that truth there can be no denial.

> The greatest of all *denials* is hiding from the fact that tough times are inevitable!

> The greatest of all *mistakes* is the belief that there will be no mistakes!

> The greatest of all *curses* is the assumption that none are coming!

> The greatest of all *disasters* is not being prepared for the next one!

I don't want you to be remiss in helping those you love and those you lead to be prepared for the good and the bad. Far too long, we may, for our own comfort, have shied away from preparing for hard times, disappointments, failures, tough choices, and making right decisions. To truly overcome, bounce back, and regroup you will need every appropriate resource available. Let's begin with three resources you will definitely need in order to prepare for, plow through, and profit from tough times: passion, skills, and strategies. A fourth resource—having and being able to tell a good story—always helps.

"*Passion is wonderful, skills are a must, but you have to have a winning strategy!*" I will never forget the first time I heard Doug Carter, Senior VP of Equip, say those words. Then, leaning forward into our small group of would be leaders, he began telling his story, "Guys it takes all three— heart (passion), hands (skills), and head (strategy)." He ought to know.

Doug Carter was born in a small, Deep South, purely segregated, rural cotton farming community. From this humble beginning, came one of the most passionate encouragers anyone has ever met. Dr. Carter has logged over three million frequent flyer miles, after serving as a missionary, VP of World Gospel Missions, and President of Ohio Christian University.

What drives this, "Let's go now!" persona?

He says it is his passion (love) for others. He has visited and lectured in over 125 countries. Just like June Bug, Doug loves to share his "quilt." He warms the heart, mind, and soul of all he meets.

But passion alone is not enough, he says. You have to know how to raise funds—his skill. Mr. Carter has raised somewhere around 100 million dollars for EQUIP, a nonprofit arm of John C. Maxwell's leadership organization. Doug literally wrote the book on his skill, *Raising More than Money: Redefining Generosity*!

But, that's not enough either, he says. You have to have a winning strategy. His strategy was to serve as a number two servant leader, and raise up a small army of four hundred or so volunteers who would pay their own way to help fulfill EQUIP's vision in 196 countries around the world; investing in the lives of six million equipped leaders.

I was privileged to teach several times for EQUIP in Ukraine and Honduras. Why? Because Doug Carter understands the balance between passion, skills, and strategies, and because he asked!

I am well aware that life's challenges can take on biblical proportions, but even those dramatic provocations were met with miraculously unvarnished passion, skills, and strategies.

Remember David and the gigantic problem, Goliath?

"David, shepherd boy what are you doing with that sling shot?"

"Practicing, practicing, practicing."

The other soldiers said, "Goliath is too big to fight."

David, the unafraid, said, "He's too big to miss."

"David, why five stones for your sling?"

"Goliath has four brothers, and I'm not aiming to miss one of them!"

Am I saying life's challenges work out smoothly every time? Absolutely not. It is the responsibility of those who love you to *stand up to you* when your passions are misplaced, *stand with you* when your skills fail, and *stand by you* when your strategies go wrong. Don't give up and don't give in.

You must have a tolerance for ambiguity and negativity. Planning for no trouble is naïve.

I recall a memorable trip to the Okefenokee Swamp Park in Waycross, Georgia. Gators, gators, gators!

There were signs everywhere that read, "Insect repellant recommended!"

The "Insect repellant recommended!" warnings were prominent on the entrance sign, the welcome sign, the front desk sign, and even on the sign we ducked under to get on the tour boat.

But we were in a hurry to catch the final ride of the afternoon through the largest black water swamp in America.

That salivating swarm of super-sized mosquitoes that attacked us realized that we were the last meal of the day.

They were not immoral or unconstitutional. They just smelled four fresh Kentuckians and said, "shall we eat'm here or tak'm home?"

We aced the passion and failed at strategy.

Rock Lesson #1

The Rocks Come with the Farm.

CHAPTER TWO

Stay in the Game

"If there are ever sermons in stones,
it is when they are built into a stone fence."
—John Burroughs

Nassim Taleb, in his book *The Black Swan*, explains the really big rocks as unlikely—but not impossible—catastrophes that no one ever seems to plan for.[1] Terrorist attacks, Hurricane Harvey, the wildfires out west, Aleppo, and Great Recessions. You must anticipate the rocks, and for the really big ones, brace for calamity, just as we insure our farm home against flood, fire, earthquakes, and violent weather.

On October 8, 2016, Hurricane Matthew blew onto Hilton Head, South Carolina's well-planned perfection, reported Travel Writer Patty Nickell. According to the article, winds of nearly 100 MPH left damages in the millions of dollars, "and one paradise that, in a nod to poet John Milton, needed to be regained!"[2]

Matthew was the first hurricane to hit Hilton Head in 126 years, yet thanks to amazing "planning for perfection" by Charles Fraser, the real estate developer and visionary of Hilton Head, and some equally amazing rapid-response cleanup efforts, Hilton Head is "once again its sun-dappled, palmetto-fringed, ocean-breeze-kissed self," reported Nickell.

Whether the call to arms is called disaster planning or planning for perfection, the trouble will be dressed in black and blue when it comes. Hilton Head planned ahead so they could stay in the game and stay in the game they did. Three weeks after Matthew, they hosted the classic car show, *Concours d'Elegance*.

On the garden plow we pull behind our John Deere tractor is a shear pin that breaks away when the plow hits a large, immovable rock—releasing the plow, saving it from severe damage, and preventing us from being catapulted off the tractor.

According to their news release, the new John Deere Starfire 6000 satellite receiver, used on their large equipment like combines, has navigation algorithms that can remotely guide and avoid obstacles like large immovable underground rocks. With an accuracy of a little more than an inch, it guarantees precise placement of seed and nutrients, avoiding costly damages and downtime.I want to be assured that you have your shear pins in place and your GPS on.Some rocks simply need to be plowed around, some moved, some crushed to be used! Some stubborn rocks—unrealized dreams, thwarted ambitions, difficult occupations, deprivations, and unreached goals—can be transformed into something useful or beautiful. Think the Grand Canyon, the Great Wall, pyramids, or Michelangelo's David. Under enough stress, coal becomes a diamond.

Stress has fifty synonyms, including agony, hardship, worry, fearfulness, trepidation, and oppression.[2] To be useful, stress needs to have at least one purpose. Cait Murphy of *Fortune Magazine* recommends praising stress (rocks), which she believes is "*essential to fitness and inevitable in life, but it's important to remember to incorporate rituals of recovery.*"

One of science's remarkable principles is that energy can be harnessed, allowing you to play, work, and accomplish twice as much as you dreamed possible.

Gregory Dixon tells how one life lost became two lives lived in his behind-the-scenes story of Russell Conwell, author of *Acres of Diamonds.*

Russell Conwell was a Civil War Hero, a graduate of Yale, a high-powered lawyer, the greatest lecturer and motivational speaker of his time, a publisher, an educator, a real estate developer and entrepreneur, pastor of the largest Protestant church in America at the time, and founder of the Good Samaritan Hospital and Temple University.

However, he and his family were no strangers to self-denial, hard labor, and poverty. Notwithstanding, a wonderful love for each other, God, and country permeated their remote home place in Massachusetts. The byproduct of this isolation was a greater focus on studies. Russell was said to have spent every spare moment reading, constantly borrowing books.

Dixon points out that he and his brother Charles endured embarrassment and overcame many frontier struggles while at the same time their character and reputations as leaders grew, even in this dimly lit corner.

At nineteen, Russell was unanimously elected as captain of his company, "Mountain Boys." He led his men out of a genuine desire to serve others. He was honored with a commemorative sword inscribed with this slogan, *True Friendship is Eternal.*

Second Massachusetts Regiment of Heavy Artillery was later formed and Conwell was again made captain. Although too young to serve, Conwell's beloved orderly, John Ring, became Conwell's personal assistant and was constantly at his side. John Ring was killed while trying to honor his hero by saving Conwell's sword from the Confederates.

War's traumatic experiences and the horrifying news of his orderly's tragic death pushed Conwell to seek some needed answers about eternal matters. Author Dixon says he accepted Christ, and was never the same again. *When I stood beside the body of John Ring and realized that he had died for love of me, I made a vow that has formed my life. I would live the life of John Ring. From that moment I have worked sixteen hours every day—eight for John Ring's work and eight hours for my own.*

According to Dixon's account a double life meant double trouble. His real estate business struggled. In 1868, everything he owned was lost in a fire. He discovered that a mysterious illness he had was actually caused by a brass bullet that he had been struck with while fighting in the war two years earlier. In 1870, he started over again as a lawyer. He made plenty of money even though he offered legal services to the poor, free of charge. Then sickness suddenly took his lovely wife. At the age of thirty-seven he made what others called a quick and extremely foolish choice that would lead to poverty and failure. He shut down his law office and real estate business, answering the call to the ministry.

I surrendered all and kept on amid the scoffs and reproaches of my best friends. And while I have seen hours of trials; met sore defeats; been wounded by jealousies; injured by misunderstandings; yet, as I look back upon my life now, I cannot see that I suffered greater hardships that I expected.

"A good name is rather to be chosen than great riches, and loving favor rather than silver and gold." Conwell, a tireless worker, was also known as a leader who was extremely efficient at accomplishing tasks and delegating authority. He knew how to appoint leaders with a keen business sense along with great organizational skills. He also knew how to get work done through others.Conwell had a secret that helped him to avoid procrastination: his "Do-It-Now" rule. An institution can never rise above the vision or qualifications of its leadership. If a need were legitimate, purposeful, and justifiable, Conwell believed that the very need itself carried the inherent and potential power to supply the answer for the need.

The founding of Temple University, still a major institution today, came about simply because a young man without money asked questions and Conwell wanted to see that he found the answers.

I haven't met a successful individual who has not read *Acres of Diamonds*; my unabridged copy is on the top shelf in the library.

Where do the round rock stone walls of Massachusetts, the white rock houses in the Texas Hill Country, and our gorgeous Kentucky limestone rock fences, fireplaces, churches, and bridges come from?

They were quarried or cleared from the fields of the farms to allow for crops, cattle, and, here in Kentucky, for the thoroughbred horses to romp free in the lush bluegrass paddocks bordered by picturesque stone fences.[3]

While observers of the American countryside may view rocks as obstacles, hindrances, or enemies, rock fence experts Carolyn Murray-Wooley and Karl Raitz are quick to point out that in the Bluegrass of Kentucky, rocks are a blessing. "Ancient limestone yielded the region's fertile soils that provided the basis for the luxuriant vegetation so admired by both the native Indians and the European explorers." These same limestones were, with no little effort and expense, quarried to provide fence material" and to make mansions of stone.

"If there are ever sermons in stones, it is when they are built into a stone wall, turning your hindrances into helps, shielding your crops behind the obstacles to your husbandry, making the enemies of the plow stand guard over its product," says John Burroughs in *Signs and Sermons.*

When you are under undue pressure, pause, pray, and remember the signature line in the biblical story of Joseph, the guy with the coat of many colors. "You meant this for harm, but God intended it for good."[4] Gerda Weissmann Klein, who survived deportation, the ghetto, three years of Nazi labor camps, and then three more months of a bitter winter 350-mile death march from the Polish-German border to southern Czechoslovakia, explains this beautifully in her book *All But My Life:*

"No manual for survival was ever handed to me, nor were any self-help books available. Yet somehow, I made my way, grappling with (my) feelings: that would let me reconcile difficult memories with hope for the future and balancing pain with joy, death with life, loss with gain, tragedy with happiness."[5]

Below are the moving words of Medal of Freedom winner Klein. Forever inscribed on one of the six center piece glass columns in the New England Holocaust Memorial in Boston.

"Ilse, a childhood friend of mine, once found a raspberry in the (concentration) camp and carried it in her pocket all day to present it to me on a leaf. Imagine a world in which your entire possession is a raspberry and you gave it to your friend."

"Such people don't come out healed . . . they come out different."[6]

It's important to prepare as best you can—to endure when you must. For twenty or so years, each Super Bowl Sunday we were privileged to hear an inspirational super sermon by Wayne B. Smith entitled, *"Playing Hurt."*

"The bottom line, Super Bowl players play hurt or they don't play. . . . whether you're on the football field or in the kitchen or in the office, you're going to be hurt. We either had problems, are having them now, or will have them. . . . stay in the game."[7]

What about the biggest comeback in the Super Bowl's history by thirty-nine-year-old Tom Brady and the Patriots?

You don't get a Super Bowl ring if you can't stay in the game. Navy Seals, Army Rangers, Commandos, elite teams, super performers, and all professional athletes play hurt, but they stay in the game.

Both my left tibia and fibula were broken in the last, now infamous, flag football game in which I ever played. Six months, three weeks, and two days in a full leg plaster cast caused me to lose the dorsa flex in my left foot. I'm out of the game . . . but nobody has a problem knowing it's me when I'm coming down the hall—step-flop, step-flop, step-flop!

I am deeply indebted to those who encouraged me to finish the game in my pursuit of a doctorate degree. Let me explain.

I remember the disappointment and countless anxious days I waited after being denied entrance to Class I, the first ever doctoral class offered at our university. Thanks to good advice and help from some fabulous relationships I was selected for Class II.

In the very first course of my doctoral studies program, the senior professor emphatically announced that of the forty students enrolled, statistically only four would graduate with a Ph.D.

He could not have shocked me more if he had dumped the customary celebratory cooler full of ice-cold Gatorade on me!

Now, you want to crush my dream and steal my joy! Never!

My resolve was steeled . . . harder than ever before.

Class after hard class, intimidations, and discouragements only made my will stronger. Four of us formed a study group for the final exam and made a promise to meet together for five hours every Saturday for six months without missing. One left the group; another did not take the exam.

Next came a year of dissertation approval and research. However, before the final steps of analysis and defense, I came out of the game.

I became preoccupied with the required move out of state, new job, new home, and a hundred new responsibilities. Including keeping a close eye on my son as he mastered the art of skidding to a complete stop, backwards, from full speed, on his Big Wheel plastic tricycle.

As the window of opportunity for submission narrowed, a dear friend, Eddie Crapps, held me accountable and forcibly reminded me of my promise and commitment! *"You're on the sidelines, get back in the game!"*

I was blessed with an empathetic support team, headed by my wife, that gave, forgave, and stuck with me down to the final question asked on dissertation defense day. I was asked to answer an inquiry that was beyond the slightest relevance to anything concerning my dissertation. Game over! My advisory professor perceived the acute panic, calmly rose and said, "I believe that perhaps I'm the only person in the room that can possibly answer that question." I left that room as a Ph.D. candidate and with a friendship that has lasted a lifetime!

I was also one of only four students to receive their Ph.D. in that Class II.

Rock Lesson #2
Stay in the Game.

CHAPTER THREE

Valley of the Angels

"Great necessities call out great virtues."
—Abigail Adams

"People with a higher degree of emotional resilience are more likely to achieve outstanding results than others. In other words, people who are able to bounce back from adversity and leverage their challenge are more likely to be top achievers in their field."[1]

These successful people know how to turn hard circumstances into profits, leadership positions, or best-sellers, and accomplish things that are just short of a miracle.

We were on our way to a South American national treasure, the Valley of the Angels in Honduras, when our guide, Jorge Pinto, Director of Montecito Orphanage, stopped our short pilgrimage to introduce us to Joeny Ordonez. The story Joeny told us that day changed my life. Although their wages were meager, he said, he and his lovely wife were fortunate starting out, he as a utility serviceman and his wife as an office worker.

Along came three beautiful kids; however, one of their daughters had a chronic kidney illness that consumed any extra monies. Without warning he lost his job. He said "everything here is political, you know!"

The financial slide was severe. They lost their home, went to a rental, lost the rental, moved in with a relative. Expenses for hospital visits mounted. With too many reversals, even their relatives' help ended.

Extreme difficulties called for desperate decisions: Mom and Dad would eat every other day so their children could eat each day.

More doctor bills, less hope . . . Still there was Friday, his wife's payday—surely they could make it. But, on her walk back home from cashing the little check, she was robbed.

He looked me straight in the eye and asked, "What would you do?"

That night, he slipped a butcher knife inside his shirt and headed for the local pay phone stand. He would rob whichever unfortunate soul came by that night.

Nine p.m. . . . no one. Ten p.m. . . . still no one.

"By eleven," Joeny said, "I was so messed up I prayed for God to send me someone to rob!"

That prayer's answer was the recall of an almost forgotten promise of hope. Months before Pastor Pinto had said, "If you ever need me, just call."Joeny's plagued mind was as dark as that dreadful, troubled Saturday night. *Did the Pastor mean it? Should I possibly call at 11:30 p.m. and ask for 100 lempira?* (Five U.S. dollars.)Pastor Pinto did answer the phone, and said, "No, not 100 lempira," but, instead, he would come immediately with 1000 lempira and food enough for the whole family.

The next morning, church members brought not only baskets of food, but much more—faith, hope, and love.

Pastor Pinto told Joeny to report to the church the next day—he had a job for him. No pay, just a job.

The job eventually included taking bottled water to the Tegucigalpa dump people.

After several visits to the dump, his ill daughter asked if she could go with him. "No!" was his repeated answer, but her persistence won, and finally she was allowed to ride along one day, then every day.

Her little heart was touched for the tiny babies sheltered in cardboard boxes, the dirty little children picking through the stinking heaps for plastic, metal, or food. It was a tragic scene . . . acres and acres of nothing but garbage, hundreds of buzzards, packs of starving dogs, and dozens of bone-skinny cows. A mad scramble ensued every time a new load of garbage arrived. Competition for the slightest of anything was dangerous.His eyes filled with tears as he told us that on this very afternoon he was to officiate the funeral of Kevin, an eleven-year-old boy who had been backed over by a garbage truck. Kevin left behind five younger siblings.Joeny's daughter began to beg for him to do something for these children. Her insistence would not stop. Finally Joeny asked Pastor Pinto what he thought of her requests to help.His answer: "I believe it to be the voice of God."

The first outreach was to be for five to ten kids to meet under the shade trees across the road from the dump to assess needs. Forty showed up!

Today, *Amor Fe Y Esperanza* (Love, Faith, and Hope) or AFE, is a life-saving ministry to the 1500 children, men, and women who live in or work daily in the gigantic refuse dump of Tegucigalpa. AFE is a constant bee hive of comfort, support, and learning activities including a nursery, kindergarten, grade school, middle, and high school. They have now sent their first graduates to college.

AFE's miracles come from East and West. They receive expert educational guidance from Harvard, no less. A well-known Las Vegas Casino owner's grandson helped them by financing a new multipurpose building. "

Yes, wonderful people have taken notice," he said, "but we need to do more; please pray for us!"

By the way, Joeny's daughter, Daniela, received expert medical help and is doing fine.

The first United States father and son presidents were both recipients of the steady guidance and wisdom of another who heard the cry. This time the call came wrapped in red, white, and blue. The desperate appeal was for independence. The response required sacrifice, loneliness, and hardship from a wife and mother.

The words of Abigail Adams in a note to teenage son John Quincy, who would become our sixth President, leaving home again, this time for years abroad, ring true still.

"Great necessities call out great virtues. When a mind is raised, and animated by scenes that engage the heart, then those qualities which would otherwise lay dormant wake into life and form the character of the hero and statesman."[2]

Rock Lesson #3

The golden opportunities are often found under the rocks of adversity.

CHAPTER FOUR

Rock Solid Decisions

What God overlooks, the paparazzi prints!

You need a solid rock to stand on in times of trouble, especially when you are forced to make a life-altering decision.

Always remember the parable of the wise and foolish builders and a house built on rock versus a house built on sand. Our solid rock decision to put family, God, and country foremost in our lives led my son, Jason, to safeguard, as best he felt he could, all three values on that fateful date of 9/11. He informed us that he was going to go active duty Army, but Mimi pleaded for him to graduate from University of Kentucky first. He was commissioned 2nd Lieutenant the day after graduation.

One of my favorite pictures shows Jason in Afghanistan, standing on that mountain of boulders with the rock houses in the background. It is a reminder of what to do any time you doubt your resolve or abilities to finish strong. Here is a copy of a commendation letter we received from Jason's commander. (Note its reference to the rocks).

It's hard to believe, that 5 years and one month ago, to the day, that I met then 2LT Jason Mitchell, the Commander of Alpha Battery 1ˢᵗ Battalion 6ᵗʰ Field Artillery. We have slipped on the same rocks on the 7000' climb to OP LOYALTY and said the same prayer crossing the Russian Bridge heading towards the ANP Checkpoint south of Dow Ab where you could always count on a fight. Like the village blacksmith in the poem by Henry Wadsworth Longfellow, Jason has and continues to serve as a role model balancing his job with the role he plays with his family and community, and as Longfellow said, "And looks the whole world in the face, for he owes not any man."

Jason took the reins of Bravo in Afghanistan providing fires in support of the entire Brigade Combat Team. Jason's battery fired over 6,000 rounds and today those Bravo noncommissioned officers and soldiers make up the resident firing expertise spread across the battalion's howitzer sections and fire direction centers.

Captain Mitchell best of luck to you and your family as you start a new chapter in your life. You will no doubt have an incredible impact.

—Col. Condrey

Jason's bronze star for leadership and dedication in combat operations under great adversity, as well as the heroic endeavors of every rock-solid service man and woman, embodies my favorite scripture: *"Greater love hath no man than this, that a man lay down his life for his friends."*[1]

Not surprisingly, there's a military process to situational analysis (moving rocks). Air Force Colonel John Boyd developed the OODA Loop, which stands for Observe, Orient, Decide, Act. Through this iterative process, military folks observe a situation, process what it means through orientation, decide on a course of action, and then act to solve the problem.[2]

When you are faced with a decision, make that decision as wisely as possible, then forget it. The moment of absolute certainty never arrives.[3]

General Colin Powell has a rule of thumb about making tough decisions—you should have no less than 40% and no more than 70% of the information you need. A key part of his rule is intuition; he says that's what separates great leaders from average leaders.[4]

How do you make the "right" decision?

Here is my model:

1. Is it good?.. The Smell Test

2. Is it legal? ....The Jail Test

3. What if it were published? ....The Newspaper Test

Let me tell you a little more about each test.

Is it good? The Smell Test: This is an informal method for determining whether something is authentic and credible by using your common sense of propriety. We have a rule in property management, and if you ever break it, you only break it once. Never open a refrigerator door in an empty house if the electric is off. The consequences of ignoring the smell test are the same as opening that door . . . sickening to all senses and to everyone around.

The smell test is enshrined in the old adage—if it's too good to be true; it's too good to be true! It is a cleverly disguised lie, a scam, inviting everyone involved to cut corners. It always takes advantage of the gullible.

Is it legal? The Jail Test: You can do anything you want to anyone you want for as long as you want—until you get caught. I am not sure, but if you listen to all the excuses given, you would think all prison stripes are some shade of gray. Few ever willingly admit wrongdoing. We need to learn what is black and white out there. My bottom line is always "what will the jury say?"

What if it were published? The Newspaper Test: Early in my real estate career someone recorded all conversations that were going on in a house I was showing; that changed my behavior forever. Never do I openly comment on their spoiled dogs or ugly children's pictures. I am careful to behave as if everything I say is being bugged, photographed, and soon-to-be hacked. What God overlooks, the paparazzi prints!

Is it ethical? The Peer Test: In every profession, there are ethics and normal standards of practice—rules of behavior that guide our interactions with clients and peers. All seem to be based on the Golden Rule. *Do unto others as you would have others do to you.* I would rather be *Chairman of,* than the *defendant before,* the Professional Standards Committee.

Four rules when you screw up: admit it, apologize, correct it, and if possible make restitution.

Be careful about burning bridges. Most acts of permanently ending relationships harshly or unpleasantly ensures you will not be welcomed back. Make sure there is no possibility you may need or want to return.

Of course, in the case of sleazy, corrupt, carnally immoral character or situations with a toxic environment the message is: exit only!

Does it make my life better? The Stress Test: What are you trading your life for? How many hours are you willing to work to pay for what you want to buy? There has to be a balance. Little stress equals little victory. Too much stress makes life *bitter,* not *better.*

The treadmill exercise stress test or electrocardiogram lets your doctor know how your heart responds to being pushed. Too elevated of a heart rate, abnormal rhythm, or a drop in the blood flow to your heart muscle are signs of possible trouble ahead.

When making decisions about doing this, going there, or buying something, ask does this really make my life better?

Does it make me money? The Profit Test: You can't go broke making a profit! However, you can find yourself in great need with too much greed! The greatest marketing plan in the world that doesn't result in a sale for you and a profit for me is a blueprint for disaster and an invitation for unhappiness.

Does it take me where I want to go? The Map Test: Thank goodness for GPS and Siri, but I still love that line, "always take the scenic route home."[5] Does this decision help me get where I really want to go?

Varun Ramakrishnan, an A+ student of mine wrote the following paper which perfectly illustrates this principle.

My dream in life is to become a surgeon. Just the thought of using my own two hands to cure another person has fascinated me since childhood. But naturally, as all young, egotistical surgeons are, I love wealth.

For the past several decades, physicians have become renaissance men, dipping their fingers in any pool of profit. I first became interested in the idea of owning a private practice in my early teens, when my uncle, a respected urologist, opened his second private practice office. In many ways, he symbolized the American dream, coming from humble beginnings to owning the finest life has to offer. To this day, he attributes his wealth to one thing: leaving academic medicine for greener pastures in private practice.

I'm a firm believer in the notion that if you wish to accomplish something, you must learn directly from the person who has what you desire. It is for this reason that early in my collegiate career, I reached out to a locally renowned bariatric surgeon who operates on severely obese individuals seeking drastic weight loss. Having naturally lost eighty pounds in high school, weight loss has always been a fascinating process to me. During my weight loss process, I met many obese individuals who were simply too heavy to lose weight safely through exercise. Often time, these individuals presented with other complications such as heart disease, diabetes, and fatty liver disease, making traditional weight loss an impossible activity for them. For these individuals, bariatric surgery was their only hope, a single opportunity to live healthy.

My new doctor friend quickly became a mentor to me, someone I could approach with my questions about medicine, wealth, and life. Previously a general surgeon in a hospital setting, he transitioned into private practice, opening one of the only bariatric clinics in the state. Over the course of several years, his clientele and reputation grew, until his team became the premier bariatric surgical group in the state. As he once fondly told me, "There was a point where I would finish a case, get on a private jet, and fly to another city for the next case."

His practice was something to admire, a large office space with multiple examination rooms, a grand waiting area with marble flooring, and a full staff of receptionists, nurses, and medical coders. It was something I could have only dreamed of. After several months of shadowing, I had convinced myself that private practice was the route for me. I had found my niche in life, to be a renowned surgeon with a thriving business (and a Porsche 911 wouldn't hurt too).

Entering your FIN360 class, I had grand ideas of becoming a physician-real estate investor hybrid. I aspired to own multiple practices and make a name for myself, not only in the medical community but in the commonwealth. As my special class project, I decided to interview my friend regarding his private practice.

I wished to learn how he started his medical empire and how I could have a slice of this pie. It was with great shock naturally, that I came to learn he had left private practice. In what ended up being a two-hour phone call, the good doctor revealed information that would change my dreams.

After nearly twenty years as a private practice physician, he decided to contract with a first-rate local hospital. The hospital would pay off the remainder of his mortgage, provide him with a generous salary, benefits, and employ his office as a satellite clinic strictly for bariatric patients. It had seemed that the strain of private practice had worn him down. While initially, the complete control he had over his practice had been appealing, he cited a desire to spend more time doing the things he loved. He wished to spend more time raising his daughter, playing tennis, and finally enjoying the fruits of his labor.

Being in control of his staff's payroll, making mortgage payments on his office, and renovating his office every few years had worn on him. He described his hospital contract with such great relief, stating how lucky he was to have a hospital assume his costs outright. It was a dramatic shift from the feelings he had conveyed to me a year earlier. I could tell by his voice how drained he had become, but also how happy he was now that he no longer was in private practice.

While some part of me will always appreciate the idea of private practice, I have become comfortable with the idea of working for a hospital with more controlled hours. Ultimately, I have tempered my expectations in medicine. While wealth is admirable and while I still plan to involve myself with real estate investment somehow, I believe my aspiration to enter private practice was misguided and shortsighted. I failed to account for all the minutiae involved with owning a clinic, instead focusing on how amazing it must feel to own one. But most importantly, I became so lost in my dream of becoming wealthy that I neglected my other dreams: of having a successful marriage, raising a family, and traveling the world with friends. I hope that through the remainder of this semester, I am able to learn more that will help guide my decisions and allow me to become an impactful surgeon, husband, father, and friend someday.

The jury is back in with a verdict on this student . . . he knows where he is going . . . to change lives!

Rock Lesson #4
Always ask, what will the jury say, then decide.

CHAPTER FIVE

The Three Biggest Rocks: Relationships, Resources and Resilience

"A crisis is a terrible thing to waste."
—Paul Romer

Mimi and I faced one of our severest map tests when the Great Recession tsunami hit the real estate market. There's no question that without our priceless relationships, invaluable resources, and old-fashioned resilience, we would not have made it through that rock-hard turn of events. The three R's saved us in tough times:

1. **Relationships** – Treasure your emotionally connected friends and trusted advisors. Make sure you have a team of business relationships. You will need a tough attorney, a talented CPA, a trustworthy financial advisor, and a turn-to-in-tough-times-banker to ensure your financial safety net.

Lesson: Make close friends and build strong relationships in all spheres of your life. Friendships are hard work. They must be nourished and prioritized properly in your busy schedule.

Relationships are the keys to the doors of every successful adventure.

Good relationships are the key to invaluable information. You are free to ask: *Who* do you know that I should know? *What* do you know that I should know? *When* do you think I should? *Where* did I go wrong and *Why*?

Great relationships are the keys to true wealth and happiness. To lift my spirits all I have to do is think of Eddie and Phyllis around their grill or in the blueberry patch. Or about my granddaughters' dear friends the Johnson girls; as well as Buster and Pam's gift horses, Ossie and Streak.

During the worst of the Great Recession, when most corporations were radically reducing costs, Gary Ermers, the Chief Financial Officer of a major hospital, announced to all that they were honoring their contractual commitments to our company. He judiciously sliced through the red tape. That was a game changer for us. When your relationships are right, right wins! That kind of CFO builds great relationships by being a person of character who never regrets or retreats from doing the right thing.

I have a very close relationship with Dr. Donald Foshee, retired Vice President at Valdosta State University.

When I was a graduate student, Dr. Foshee asked me if I would like to teach a Psychology 101 class. I immediately said, "Yes!"

However, after realizing how much work my talented teacher-wife did every day gathering resources, preparing lesson plans, and developing strategies, I got scared to death. I thought, *I can't do this!* Finally, I expressed my fears and apprehensions to Dr. Foshee. Without hesitation he looked me straight in the eye and said, "Teaching Psychology 101 takes 5 percent genius and 95 percent bull*#*%. You are perfect for the job."

I have been teaching ever since.

2. **Resources** – Have a strong faith in God, family, and our country.

Lesson: Continually build your faith. Invest in your family daily. I love the fact that my granddaughters never say goodbye without adding, "I love you." Let your pledge of allegiance be your solemn oath.

3. **Resilience** – Each "no" simply means that you have uncovered another way that doesn't work.

Lesson: Have a plan B. Never stop learning or reading. Turn off the TV and take out those ear phones.

Adopt the old adage, "A crisis is a terrible thing to waste." Replenish your storehouse of knowledge, revisit options, and reboot your business. I describe it as keeping your pot hot!

I still teach a class at the University of Kentucky, though some may not know why. I teach because those bright, young minds challenge me. They don't want to know what worked "back in the day." They want to know what will make them successful in the future.

As soon as the recession hit the sale of homes, we added a property management company. A builder friend of mine's plan B was to travel the state finishing out incomplete repossessed homes for a large bank. Other builders became top-notch remodelers.

Rock Lesson #5

Your Plan B must redefine rejection; refocus past the rock slide to the rewards up ahead.

CHAPTER SIX

Ole Shep

Heroes respond instantly, instinctively, and unselfishly!

We are all wired with seven response emotions: anger, fear, disgust, contempt, joy, sadness, and surprise. These are thermometers, not thermostats. One reveals; the other regulates. These emotional filters affect how we hear, see, and feel when faced with overly sensitive experiences.

Like everyone says in the School of Hard Knocks, crisis doesn't make your character—it reveals it.

Be sure to fill the deepest reservoirs of your mind and heart with humility, simplicity, restraint, dedication, faith, and perseverance. Your default responses will automatically be transparent, accountable, and genuine.

I can still see the sweat pouring off the faces of June Bug and my cousins, Pearlie, Wilkie, Billy Ray, Marston,

Minnie, Wanda, Darlene, and Little Ike, as the noisy pulley lowered the two-foot-long, galvanized water bucket down into Aunt Vera's well. At that moment, we forgot how long the rows in the garden were or how hot the day. We always knew what was coming—cold, refreshing, clear spring water. Each of us, the biggest first down to the littlest, would fill the dipper made from a colorful gourd until it was running over. We drank every drop.

Since there are no perfect people, since life is not altogether fair, and since no one is always right, you would seemingly be at a moral disadvantage to those that lie, cheat, and steal! It is precisely for this reason and at those times you must stand like a rock!

Sweat a little bit; maybe, but never waver when your integrity, honesty, convictions, and positive focus are on the line.

All partnerships and all friendship have three members: you, your partner, *and* trouble! But the partnerships and friendships that overcome trouble are successful, lasting, and make wonderful historic things happen.

Let me share a story about how one of my dearest mentor's "best friend" handled his relationship problem.

Harry W. Blackburn was perhaps the most magnificent orator I have ever had the privilege of knowing and calling a friend. He gave me permission to "forever share" his story. His audiences never forgot it, yet always insisted he tell "Ole Shep" again and again.

As a boy, Harry and his brother lived in the plains of Kansas on a hard-working, wind-swept crop farm. He said their home was modest, filled with stern love, lit by coal oil, and always smelled of home-cooked, hearty meals.

Ole Shep was mostly bulldog with a big wrinkled, white and tan face, no neck, square jaw, sad, sad eyes, two big buck teeth sticking straight up, and slobbers everywhere. No one knew what the other parts were. Mr. Blackburn, Sr., always said "just dog, I guess."

Ole Shep was very protective. No opossum, armadillo, or pocket gopher lived long if they ventured too close to the Blackburn place.

Even the mailman would yell, "Now, Mr. Blackburn, you better control that dog or no mail today!"

Only on rare occasions when mother needed sugar or flour were Harry and his brother allowed to take the horse and buggy to town, but never was Ole Shep allowed to tag along.

One fine autumn day, the brothers heard those sweet words, "Boys, I need . . ." They ran and tied up Ole Shep and headed toward town, whistling loudly, enjoying their freedom, and anticipating some store-bought candy. They were just a mile from town before they noticed that Ole Shep was right behind the wagon, with his hind quarters and stubby little tail just a-wagging.

Harry grabbed the buggy whip to make him go back home, but his brother said, "No, you can't. It's too late. If we make him go back, he'll take the shortcut across the train trestle over the river and fall through or be run over. He'll just have to fend for himself."

By the time they tied up at the general store they had forgotten about Ole Shep . . . until they heard the barking, howling, yapping, and general dog cussing of the local canine pack. Here they came—old hounds and young pups, big dogs, little dogs, fat dogs, skinny dogs, long-haired dogs, no-haired dogs, mean looking dogs, one-eyed dogs, dumb dogs, cold dogs, and hot dogs. All with bad intentions.

When that posse rounded the corner onto Main Street, they were almost close enough to smell Ole Shep's bad breath. Some little runt of a canine scampered between the big, bad lead dog's legs. Ole Shep took one swipe and removed him from contention.

Harry started to jump down, but his brother held him back. "It's up to Ole Shep now," he said.

Ole Shep never took another step. He planted those four oversized paws deep into that Kansas dust. He swelled his chest and squared his shoulders. Every muscle from head to toe was rock solid. In embarrassing disruption, every dog simultaneously slammed on the brakes, though not quick enough for all. Two rolled through the chaos, took one close look at Ole Shep, and turned tail and ran. Ole Shep's eyes were blood red, but not once did he take them off the biggest, baddest dog in that pack.

Harry could hear Ole Shep's loud, deep breath of fire through his flared nostrils. He was saying things in a guttural language that no church-going Methodist should hear. It was do or die!

What happened next is what can happen when we come face to face with life's ugliest challenges.

In telling this wonderful story, Dr. Blackburn would pause, raise both arms toward heaven, never look down and start quoting from the Book of Isaiah, and in that moment you could almost hear the Hallelujah Chorus. Just for good measure he added a dozen of his other favorite scriptures, ending with, "Yea, though I walk through the valley of the shadow of death I will fear no evil . . . thou art with me."[1]Returning to his story, Harry said the leader of that pack understood perfectly who was going to win this life or death matchup.

Anger dissolved instantly, hate disappeared completely and as sweetly as the pack could, they spoke in harmony, "Hello, new friend! Welcome to town! We know where there's a juicy bone buried. Won't you kindly join us? We would love to show you around." Off the canine parade went with Ole Shep as Grand Marshal!

I have had the privilege of meeting only one recipient of the Medal of Honor, Corporal Dakota Meyer of the Marine Corps. His citation stirs the soul:

For conspicuous gallantry and intrepidity at the repeated risk of his life above and beyond the call of duty as a member of Marine Embedded Training Team 2-8, Regional Corps Advisory Command 3-7, in Kunar Province, Afghanistan, on 8 September 2009. When the forward element of his combat team began to be hit by intense fire from roughly 50 Taliban insurgents dug-in and concealed on the slopes above Ganjgal village, Corporal Meyer mounted a gun-truck, enlisted a fellow marine to drive, and raced to attack the ambushers and aid the trapped Marines and Afghan Soldiers. During a six hour fire fight, Corporal Meyer single-handedly turned the tide of the battle, saved 36 Marines and soldiers and recovered the bodies of his fallen brothers. Four separate times he fought. . . . to escape likely death at the hands of numerically superior and determined foe. On his first foray his lone vehicle drew machine gun, mortar, rocket grenade and small arms fire while he rescues five wounded soldiers . . . despite being wounded, he made a fourth attack with three others to search for missing team members. Nearly surrounded and under heavy fire, he dismounted the vehicle and searched house to house to recover the bodies of his fallen team members. By his extraordinary heroism, presence of mind amidst chaos and death, and unselfish devotion to his comrades in the face of great danger,

Corporal Meyer reflected great credit upon himself and upheld the highest traditions of the Marine Corps and the United States Naval Service.

Reading through other Medal of Honor recipients' citations one quickly observes that they all have at least three traits in common. Each and every one responded *instantly*, *instinctively*, and *unselfishly* in their hour of heroism.

Our reactions can be life-saving for ourselves and others. The gemstone standard for initial assessment in all healthcare emergencies is ABCDE which stands for Airway, Breathing, Circulation, Disability, and Exposure. The health care professionals immediately focus on the most life-threatening clinical problems.[2]

If only this process had been followed when my mother was choking in a restaurant. The patrons immediately responded as if she were having a heart attack when she really needed the Heimlich maneuver to be applied. Sad to say, but that unintentional lack of appropriate response was fatal. By the time paramedics arrived, she was gone.

To be a compassionate and life-saving first responder, have your skillset packed and ready. Know your ABCs—when your expertise is easily identifiable, when you turn mundane activities into something that is unforgettable, and when you have a shocking level of responsiveness that comes from doing things in minutes when others take days, it can be the difference between life and death.

Rock Lesson #6

When you recognize danger, incompetence, frustration, and turmoil, and you adjust instantly... You get to position yourself with the leaders.

GALLERY

Author and June Bug (oldest) in front of the Mitchell General Store
Roxana, Ky holding tax assessor black board

Part of The Mitchell Clan Cornelia, Old Jonah Mitchell, June Bug
and Caroline Back row. Author in the front.

Crazy Horse Monument Black Hills, South Dakota

Scott Co Kentucky Limestone Church & Rock Fence

The Rock Entrace on the Mitchell Farm

*Senior Class Homecoming Queen (Mimi), Author with
broken leg and best friend, Don Barchus*

Author at Shaker Village of Pleasant Hill

Jason Mitchell in Afghanistan

Caitlin (sitting) and Aubrey Mitchell climbing rocks on Mitchell Farm

CHAPTER SEVEN

Four Myths Not in the Rock Manual

*Happy, hungry people are the ones who check their
order before leaving the drive-thru.*

Here are four pea gravel-sized, tiny rock myths not
included in the geological rocks manual of correct responses:

Myth 1. You must leave no stone unturned. Every
field does not have to be plowed. Learn how to say *no*!
No to the abuse of prescription drugs. No to recreational
drugs, tobacco, and alcohol. I have never used any of these
in my entire life!

How do you keep from rear-ending the car in front of
you? It's called "assured, clear distance." Morality is keeping that distance. Almost all moral collapses are failures to

maintain assured clear distance in three areas: sex, money, and power.

You don't have to go looking for trouble . . . its coming! So, steer clear. Think Titanic. Safe speed may be greater or less than the actual legal speed limit depending upon the conditions along the road.

June Bug almost killed our sister, Caroline, when their game of roll-a-rock got out of hand. June Bug, on top of the hill, would find round rocks and roll them down the hill. Little sister Caroline's job was to beat the rocks to the bottom. The rocks got bigger, and by rock law, faster, until . . . you guessed it. Caroline wasn't quite fast enough. Bruised and crying, Caroline broke off a big switch and climbed back up that hill faster than a wildcat and madder than a swarm of angry hornets.June Bug forever insisted it was not true that she whipped him to within an inch of his life.

But the reality is he never, ever picked up a rock of any size around your Aunt Caroline again.

Myth 2. Brute strength can move any rock!

You cannot succeed with physical strength alone. It takes teamwork. It takes clear communication, shared vision, and respect. The team's respect of you and your respect of your team.

RJ Corman, of railroad fame and business, showed me the pictures of his first hours in New Orleans immediately after Hurricane Katrina. His team was removing mountains of debris, even barges washed ashore by the storm. The picture I remember most showed five or six heavy duty bulldozers, large pieces of railroad track equipment, and men operating in near waist-high mud. Seeing my astonishment, he flashed his famous grin and said, "The key is to never have all of them stuck at the same time."Don't let what you think you *cannot* do, keep you from doing what you *can*. Think of St. Jude Hospital, Save the Children, and Dream Factory.The first wish the Lexington Dream Factory granted was to a precious five-year-old, cute-as-a-button girl, with braided pigtails and thick glasses. All she wanted as her dream was the Bouncy Bee musical software so that when she left the pediatric cancer ward she could have her very own Bouncy Bee to sing along with in the comfort of her own home in Jackson, Breathitt County, Kentucky.

Thanks to the gracious people who gave the money and time, and a talented Lexmark engineer, her dream came true. When that computer went live she pressed her face close to the screen and screamed, "Bouncy Bee! It's *me*, Sissy!" No computer screen on earth ever received more hugs and kisses.

Myth 3. There are "too many" rocks on my farm.

Be careful about looking over the fence too often. *Dances with Wolves*, one of my favorite movies, has a memorable line: "This is my post; this is my post, unload this wagon, I'm stayin'!"

Wherever you find yourself that is your time, your opportunity, your challenge.

Resilient people know three things:

- To give 100 percent. Nothing more, but nothing less.

- That trying times are not the times to quit trying.

- To finish strong—this is your commitment.

Myth 4. No one cares enough to check for rocks anymore.

Happy, hungry people are the ones who check their order before leaving the drive-thru. I saw a study that found about half of both men and women still check the expiration date before purchasing their bread and milk. Your ideas, lessons, and speeches must be fresh and from the heart! Or both you and your audiences will suffer for it. *Give me a bite and I know what the whole loaf tastes like.*

I doubt anyone outside the extended family of her eight children raised on Muddy Branch in Eastern Kentucky ever ate my Grandma Cornelius Hogg Mitchell's homemade-from-scratch buttermilk biscuits. Golden brown top and bottom, two inches thick, flaky, and steaming hot from her wood-fired oven! When you split those delicious biscuits open, steam would melt the home-churned butter and the fresh Lodi apple cinnamon jelly would spread itself!

My grandma's biscuits have no equals for three reasons. *First*, careful planning provided her with the freshest and finest ingredients with which to cook. Fresh eggs were gingerly gathered from under a laying hen every morning. She only used locally grown and milled flour sold in a beautifully patterned fifty-pound flour sack, which would soon become some little granddaughter's dress. Of course there was plenty of fresh buttermilk, hand-churned by grandchildren with too much energy to waste. The *second* reason her biscuits were world-class was that they were made by someone whose heart was full of love for those kids and grandkids. She was serving up more than biscuits and gravy. The *third* reason my grandma's biscuits have no equal is that they were made for a hungry bunch by hands that served willingly. Grandma would swing us on the porch swing, work us, 'whoop' us, hug us, sing to us, but when we were hungry, she knew how to feed us with the very bread of life.

She loved us and we loved watching her from our perch on the kindling box behind the woodstove. I can still see that big crock bowl with a blue stripe around it, that porcelain countertop cabinet with a flour sifter. Mimi and I are privileged to still have her rolling pin and wooden butter mold with its hand-carved flower design.

If you inspire, you'll receive a standing ovation. A goal of our company is to receive at least one unsolicited thank you every day. This serves two purposes, it takes the edge off the inevitable criticisms and having made a difference in someone's life each day is rewarding, guaranteeing personal fulfillment and satisfaction.

Rock Lesson #7

If you inspire, you'll receive a standing ovation.

SECTION II

How to Plow Through Tough Times

CHAPTER EIGHT

The Rocks Don't Care

Success is often found in the same tough places
that created the need for it.

Plowing through is all about what happens within the soul when our pride is hurt, our happiness is disturbed, or failure is threatening.

"*Nothing stops the man who desires to achieve. Every obstacle is simply a course to develop his achievement muscle. It's a strengthening of his powers of accomplishment.*"[1]

Booker T. Washington once said, "I have learned that success is to be measured not so much by the position that one has reached in life as by the obstacles which he has overcome while trying to succeed."[2]

The key to ensuring success is often found in the same tough places that created the need for it. Leaders possess a unique spirit that, when allowed to flourish, proves its ability to take on, and overcome, any tough time. You want to know how to keep plowing through rocks? Reach deep into your mountain heritage of ingenuity, drive, courage, and plain ol' hard work. There, among your settled priorities, you'll find your strength. Since you are going to stumble, fall, and fail then always be stumbling, falling and failing forward!

Michael Jordan said it plainly: "*I've missed more than 9000 shots in my career. I've lost almost 300 games. Twenty-six times I've been trusted to take the game-winning shot and missed. I've failed over and over and over again in my life. And that is why I succeed.*"[3]

I can tell you how *not* to clear a field of rocks or win a championship game:

> Get mad
>
> Get sad
>
> Get to cussin'
>
> Get to blamin'

Don't blame the rim when you miss the shot. Every basketball coach knows that each player is given three opportunities to recognize his or her weaknesses:

1. In the mirror . . . see, you always pivot right.

2. By the coach, person in authority . . . I need you to go left.

3. The other team and everyone in the stands . . . he's going to go right, nail him!

Remember, the rocks don't care!

They simply exist as countless blessings; opportunities to release trapped works of art; bedrock for our highways; pillars for an ancient coliseum or they simply exist for our happiness, like those little flat rocks we skipped across the smooth still waters of Lake Cumberland.

I wish with all my heart that I could go with you every step of your wonderful journey, but the universal truth is you need to make your own contributions, realize your own accomplishments, and fulfill your own dreams.

What is it that Mark Batterson says? *"If your dream doesn't scare you, it's too small!"*[4]

Let me tell you of a dream come true. Mimi and I tried for a long, long time to have a baby . . . with nothing happening! We visited doctors, followed rituals, and prayed daily. After seven long years, we were at wit's end. "Let's try adoption." Another two years of forms, legal papers, and visits went by until one cold night in Atlanta your Mimi and I stopped at an outside drive-up pay phone booth (yes, they existed). Like one of those bad movies, it was dark and raining. I was outside; Mimi was leaning out the car window listening to every disappointing word coming from the Georgia Department of Family and Children Services. No, they could not be of any help at this time. Cold and discouraged, we decided to warm up in the lobby of one of the big downtown hotels. There we discovered a room full of payphones. So, we proceeded to call every adoption agency in the yellow pages. Each agency gave the same answer: no babies available for adoption. Five agencies, ten agencies, fifteen agencies . . . no, no, no.

Dispirited and defeated, we slipped into a private corner of that big hotel lobby, Mimi softly crying, and I was crushed that I could not move this rock.A well-dressed gentleman walked by us ever so slowly, returning moments later to pass right by us again. I said, "I've seen that guy before." Mimi said, "He was in the phone booth room making calls."

He returned a third time, stopped directly in front of us, dropped to one knee, and, putting his hand gently on Mimi's shoulder, said, "God has everything under control. You are going to have a baby boy."

We had come looking for an answer, and there he was. He touched our souls, and warmed our hearts.He said he was staying the night in town because a snowstorm had cancelled his flight to his home city.

He asked us if we were going to stay that night. I said, "We can't afford to stay here." He said, "There is a very special rate for college students." He invited us to join him for dinner . . . a five-course dinner, violin and all. We ate magnificent food, laughed (this is where I learned to use a finger bowl), and enjoyed his unpretentious company.He wondered if we had ever visited the shops in underground Atlanta. We told him no, but I didn't have a winter coat anyway. He loaned me his. We fell asleep that night believing in a miracle. Though we tried many times, we never, ever, spoke to him again. We were unable to contact him in any way to tell him the good news. The dream came true . . . his name is Jason.

Rock Lesson #8

Since you are going to stumble and fail, always be stumbling and failing forward.

CHAPTER NINE

Five Dirty Little Secrets of Success

*The problem with milking a cow is that the
cow won't stay milked. It's hard work being successful.*

My son, Jason, and I visited the astonishing Mt.
Rushmore and were awe-struck at its grandeur
and down-right heart-stopping size. I don't know which
was bigger—our American pride or that piece of granite!

At the same time, and not too far away, we were privileged to discover the Crazy Horse Monument. Sculptor
Korczak Ziolkowski and Lakota Chief Henry Standing
Bear officially started carving the Crazy Horse Memorial
on June 3, 1948. The memorial's mission is to honor the
culture, tradition, and living heritage of North American
Indians. Their children's children hope to finish the monument in another 70 or so years. The leadership has refused

government monies; they want to complete the project themselves! Why not?! Some things just take 150 years!

Nothing that is truly great can be accomplished in our lifetime, says Reinhold Niebuhr, "Therefore, we must be *saved by hope*. Nothing that is true or beautiful or good makes complete sense on any one day of history; therefore, we are *saved by faith*. Nothing we do, however virtuous, can be accomplished alone; therefore, we are *saved by love*."[1]

Tuck these next thoughts away in your 150-year plan. You're going to need them.

The Five Dirty Little Secrets of Success

Success contains within its very nature: distraction, mismanagement, exhaustion, emptiness, and enslavement.

Let me explain.

1. *Distraction* means by necessity there will be deferred maintenance; legitimate issues get ignored unintentionally; other lesser issues get disregarded completely. Take strong stands on very few issues. Save your emotion for the big ones. Set broad themes instead of narrow goals that can be self-defeating.

Lesson: Pay attention to the important; keep the main thing the main thing; it's not the trivial many—it's the vital few!

2. *Mismanagement* means you can't lead if you can't manage. For the sake of your leadership ego, you can't bench all of your best players. What is that law of leadership our friend and college classmate John C. Maxwell teaches? Ten percent of life is making decisions. Ninety percent of life is managing the ones you make![2]

Lesson: Pay attention to your best people often. Pay them very well.

3. *Exhaustion* means "get real." Denial is fatal.

Successful people get tired and are tempted with money, sex, power, and self-reliance! You will be severely tested by the sharks and tormented by the baby piranhas.

It was probably during one of my 5:30 a.m. early milking chores that Uncle Ike taught me that the problem with milking a cow is that the cow won't stay milked. It's hard work being successful. A successful marriage complicates your life. Wealth complicates your taxes, and success complicates your schedule! Kids and grandkids complicate your emotions, trust me. This happens to me every time Aubrey looks up with those gorgeous eyes. As she has said, "Papa you spoil us, don't you . . . but in a good way!"

Lesson: Be accountable to whoever loves you enough to say you need a break!

4. *Emptiness* means never to forget what I call the 95-5 rule. Even if you balance the 95 percent right but neglect the vital 5 percent, that little rock slide can crush your deal or really hurt your feelings.

I believe it was great-great-great-uncle George Washington Mitchell (his real name) that my grandfather said sat atop a gigantic rock bigger than an SUV with only a short-handled sledge hammer and a well-worn pick chisel. He would strike chisel marks around the stress point of that great rock and then with one precise vital blow, you could hear those ancient atoms fracture, "Crack!" He split that rock in two.

Learn quickly your stress points and guard against overreacting to criticism. There are customers you should refer. The soft "no" that I use is, *we are not your best answer.* **Lesson:** The most healing word I know is *next*!

5. *Enslavement* means you are to be a servant, but not a slave. Successful people know that time is sacrificed . . . from you, your spouse, and your kids. Some relationships unfortunately have to be minimized and too many intimate moments are lost. But we must arbitrarily and capriciously take time out for our kids, grandkids, and great-grandkids.

I loved it when we cranked up the Righteous Brothers' *Unchained Melody* CD, vibrating the windows and rocking the house as our granddaughters danced all over the fireplace room choreographing every beat!

On that same album, the Righteous Brothers also recorded "Blue Birds over the White Cliffs of Dover." This popular WWII anthem was written to lift the spirits of the Allies during the horrible, unrelenting blitz bombing of England. Only their indomitable spirit embodied in Prime Minister Winston Churchill and his powerful words "you shall go no further" stood between victory and defeat! The song looked beyond those dreaded and deadly days and nights to a time when peace would rule again!

The lyrics, "*and Jimmy will go to sleep in his own little room again,*" caused me to think of my granddaughters' multiple moves and long absences from their dad and us, but it also reminded me of their resilience, their trust in each other, and their constant love for their Mimi and me.

They have learned to deal with the "*small indelible scars by realizing the moments of pain are replaced by days of immense joy!*"[1] What wisdom and strength of character Caitlin showed when she proclaimed, "God has given me a second chance and I'm going to make the most of it!"

Lesson: Be sure to take time to make lasting memories when given a chance.

Tough times give us an opportunity to beat defeat.

I can think of no better illustration on how to beat defeat than the story of my friend, Don Crooks. Crooks was the leader of the pack, you know, class president, lovely girlfriend, destined to be most successful. At 6 foot 3, he watched over us, whipped everybody in basketball scrimmages, and to this very day is a marvelous speaker and internationally recognized teacher.

In his case, the rocks came after years of study, degrees, and grooming for a college presidency, or at least, a top denominational leadership position. However, his undeniable beliefs and personal core principles got in the way. He chose to stay true to his convictions. The tenets of his faith and doctrine cost him and his family dearly.

He wasn't run out of town, tarred, and feathered like Homer Stokes, the Reform Candidate, in *Oh, Brother, Where Art Thou . . .* , but the treatment he received was, at least, unkind, unnecessary, and extremely hurtful.

When we reconnected years later, he was teaching in a large University and was heavily involved in leadership training. His soul was at peace with that bitter chapter. Amazed I asked, "How could this be?" Here is his story.

Whether it was a dream, revelation, upset stomach, or vision, "I don't know," he said, "But what I saw, and the lesson I learned changed my attitude, my relationships, and probably saved my life.

In my vision, I saw an egg with a fully developed baby chick inside. I have learned since that as the unhatched chick develops, it begins to peck at the inside of the egg for nutrition. Eventually, this pecking at the inner coating cracks the shell. Depending on how you look at it, either the chick's world is cracked wide open or the egg bursts with opportunity that allows the baby chick to hatch.

This newfound freedom leaves the weak and somewhat confused chick with lots of choices and unlimited potential. At the same time, where is that comfortable, familiar, safe place of limited responsibilities? The only place I've known since conception.

The chick knows it is impossible to return back into the shell. That's not an option. Death is certain. The shell was a place of restricted potential and limited opportunity. This new world is frightening and chaotic with new adventures at every turn.

The chick in my vision knew there was no way back. The only choice was to embrace this new wonderful world!

A question arose in my revelation . . . what was the chick's attitude toward the cracked shell to be?

It was to be one of love and appreciation. This is where I was conceived. That incubation will forever be part of me. Though I cannot go back, I am thankful for the opportunity to be here, newborn, free, and with unlimited opportunities.

From that moment, all animosity left. I felt forgiven, I forgave.

Too often we complain about tough times instead of harnessing their energy and creating something different, helpful, and wonderful.

Turn your rocks into:

Fireplaces – write a book.

Rock fences – learn a new skill.

Masterful works – create.

Sidewalks – go serve others.

Churches – speak up for a cause.

Bookends – read!

William Hutchinson Murray said, ". . . there is one elementary truth, the ignorance of which kills countless ideas and splendid plans: that the moment one definitely commits oneself, then Providence moves too. I have learned a deep respect for one of Goethe's couplets:

Whatever you can do, or dream you can, begin it. Boldness has genius, power, and magic in it."[2]

The person who said opportunity only knocks once should be dug up and shot! Opportunity is like a bus . . . there's another one every 30 minutes. The challenge is getting on the bus that takes you where you want to go! The real danger is in not turning over the right rocks, not recognizing the gemstones, not appreciating the possibilities.

Rock Lesson #9
Successful people don't run on empty, they keep a reserve.

SECTION III

How to Profit from Tough Times

CHAPTER TEN

Things I Learned About Rocks the Hard Way

Failure is not always bad; sometimes it is bad, sometimes
it is inevitable, and sometimes it is good.

The following six retailored principles of Ancient Cicero have guided me through the tough times.[1]

1. I have learned to not worry about things that can't be changed or corrected . . . I am going to concentrate on my strengths, not my weaknesses.

Failure is not always bad, sometimes it is bad, sometimes it is inevitable, sometimes it is good.

2. I have learned to set aside trivial preferences for things of permanent good . . . I will care enough to change.

It's not always about being right . . . it's how you sleep when you go to bed tonight.

3. My individual advancement will not be made by crushing others . . . I greet this day with a great attitude in my heart.

As the song says,

"*I hear babies cry; I watch them grow.*

They'll (You'll) learn much more than I'll ever know.

And I think to myself, 'What a wonderful world.'

Yes, I think to myself, 'What a wonderful world.[2]

You must have a servant's heart. Always ask, "What can I do to help?"

4. I will not insist a thing is impossible because I cannot accomplish it . . . I have learned to be a better team member and to inspire others. It also helps to have a big brother. We often played the marble game "poison" under the majestic pines, next to the large log chapel at Buckhorn Children's Home. Some bigger boys took my drawstring bag of marbles, including my big green cat's eye shooter.

Up steps June Bug and says just one word: "Keepsies!" which means "boys, we're gonna play for keeps!" We won every round!

I walked away from that game with both front pockets of my bib overalls full of marbles.

5. I will not neglect to develop or to refine my mind, nor forget the habit of reading and studying daily.

At any given time, I am reading several books, not to mention trade magazines and articles of interest. Light content recommended books for recreational reading, interesting informative books to keep me sharp, and serious in-depth books like biographies and historical chronicles because I need to know. Which book is chosen depends on available time and my energy level. I never travel without a book or two.

6. I will not be compelled by others to believe or to live as they do . . . I will exercise great confidence in myself and in my faith.

It appears to be an apparent contradiction, why and how tough times can make you stronger, better, more confident in yourself and your faith.

Many a recess at Smootcreek School near Whitesburg was spent sitting atop a four-plank wooden fence with our backs to the school and feet a-dangling, wondering whose cars and trucks were coming down the road. Did they drive up through Mayking or down from Isom? Were they coal miners or loggers? From Ohio or Michigan? Someone would say, "They'll never make it past the Trail of the Lonesome Pine Gap up Black Mountain if they are going to Cumberland."

Everyone wondered. *If they go that way you think they'll stop at Haddie Hogg's Store? Could they be relatives coming in for the weekend? Where did they get all that money to buy such a fancy car?* But most of all, we just wondered why we couldn't be taken away from that mountain home for misplaced little lives.

Lives framed with sad countenances and feelings numbed by harsh discipline. No one ever forgot the wood-shed whoopin' of the third grader who tried to run away! Strap or woodshed were the only words needed to restore law and order.

As with all kids, we sometimes preferred tales and folk-lore to substantiate truth. I was captured by the belief that if you caught a leaf before it hit the ground from the particularly big sycamore tree in the schoolyard growing right next to Kings Creek you would get to go home! I had just caught mine, still tender enough to fold. I put it in my pocket just as the bell rang.

We were seated in rows by class. The row closest to the wall of windows was sixth graders, next fifth graders, all the way down to first grade along the back wall. Even six rows away I could not believe what I was seeing: my dad's green panel truck that he used to peddle wholesale candy was slowing down directly in front of the school.

I jumped to my feet and yelled, "There's my daddy, there's my daddy!" and headed for the door; only to be restrained by both my teacher and June Bug. Through my tears, rage, and disbelief they tried to explain that it was not my dad's truck but one that looked like it, and it was stopping at the store across the road from the school. June Bug took me back to my seat, calmed me and whispered, "soon, very soon."

I wiped away the tears with a sleeve and I slipped the other hand in my pocket to squeeze my leaf as tight as I could and believed. *Soon, very soon.*

Rock Lesson #10

It's not always about being right . . . it's how you sleep when you go to bed tonight.

CHAPTER ELEVEN

The Law of Discounting

*The most appreciated compliment is to be recognized,
the ultimate desire is to be appreciated.*

I call it the Law of Discounting when we dismissively minimize a God-given opportunity, positive or negative.

There are at least five reasons why we discount too aggressively life's opportune moments.

1. We miss the *meaningfulness*.

2. We don't properly appreciate the *source*.

3. We consider it a *distraction*.

4. We *can't recognize* it because of our fears, opinions, or prejudices.

5. We are *overpowered* by the situation.

1. Meaningfulness

Albert and Belle Blanton were kind of lost while visiting campus. I simply asked if I could help since I was headed in their direction anyway. Our friendship lasted for decades. One day on Mockingbird Lane, in their hometown, Albert said an acquaintance of his was starting a new chicken sandwich place and would I like to invest or get involved? I was too busy and too broke. Now, every time I order an 8-nugget meal at Chick-fil-A, I cry!

What if that gorgeous brunette hostess at Noel's King Boy had said no when I asked her to share my chocolate milk shake? Hello, Mimi! The lesson is: Turn down the meaningless "noise," and turn up the meaningfulness receptors.

2. Source

If it's bad news . . . cautiously consider the source and generally cut it in half. If it's good news . . . carefully consider the source and double down on paying attention. If you don't know if it's good or bad news, that's when you *really* need to pay attention. It's time to concentrate and focus!

Here are three small episodes of *good news-bad news* and dinner reservations. The first was at our Chamber of Commerce's most important event of the year. We were told on arrival that they could not find our reservations. After a few anxious moments the coordinator said, "I'm so sorry you will have to take the only two remaining seats, directly in front of the podium." Guess whose picture ended up on the front page of the paper the next morning, shaking hands with Ronald Reagan. Yes, President Ronald Reagan.

The second *good news-bad news* mix-up was at the annual National Speakers Association's Grand Gala in San Francisco. Our reservations got mixed up somehow and the only two seats the kind event planners could find for us were at one of the celebrity guest tables. We spent the evening with Og Mandino, famous author of *The Greatest Salesman in the World*, a world-wide best seller.

The third could have been a really bad news day. It involved a delicious lunch on a scenic rock ledge and guns!

I came up with what I thought was a fantastic the idea to have a picnic lunch on a gorgeous two-hundred-foot-high outcropping overlooking the sheer rock palisades of the Kentucky River. The only problems were: we had no public place to park, had to cross a busy curvy road, climb over a guard rail, and gently crawl down an embankment. The view was breathtaking. The sun was shining bright, the food was great! I thought it was romantic. Mimi thought it was downright dangerous. She was right, but the danger was not to be found on the ledge. We had parked in the corner of what I thought was an abandoned rock quarry next to an enormously large stone house. The trouble started as we were returning to our car. We were stopped cold in our tracks looking down the business end of a Kentucky long rifle. The very serious and upset owner of that gun and stone quarry had recently been robbed of several priceless antique guns. That's not all, come to find out he really knew how to use that expensive collector's rifle. He was none other than one of the world's foremost experts on military arms weaponry, Colonel George M. Chinn. Mimi says I started profusely apologizing for everything I had done wrong since childhood and never stopped talking until the Colonel finally put down his gun. It took a bit more explaining and a lot more apologizing, but we eventually became the good friends of an amazing twentieth century Renaissance man and his lovely wife, Cotton.

Colonel George M. Chinn's story captured in *Kentucky Maverick* reads like an outrageous tale, except that it is true. The Colonel was born on a mountain of rocks, afraid of nothing. He was a member of the 1921 National Championship Centre College football team that beat Harvard 6-0. He served as a bodyguard to Kentucky Governor A.B. 'Happy' Chandler. He dynamited a cave out of his family's mountain property big enough to house a diner that also served as an underground gambling operation and bar during prohibition times. He was a proud decorated Marine Corps officer and a genius military weapons designer during World War II, Korea, and Vietnam. Recipient of many awards including the Navy's highest civilian honor, the Navy Meritorious Public Service Award.

Most of his life, he was too heavy, but everything he did was bigger than life. The front door to his stone home was made from his own saw-milled walnut trees, weighed six-hundred pounds, and swung on bank-vault hinges. The open stairwell to the second floor warped around behind a massive stone fireplace. The home's rear wall was the cliff from which he quarried his stone. It's true you can profit from tough times. I had the privilege of doing project work with the Colonel on his historic stone home.

It's a good thing that this bad thing turned out to be a good thing!

The lesson is: Always ask: What good thing is possible here?

3. Distraction

When you are privileged to hear someone's story, stay focused, pick an eye, and really listen.

Aldous Huxley says, "To travel is to discover that everyone is wrong about other countries. The philosopher, the civilizations which seem at a distance, so superior to those current at home, all prove on a close inspection to be in their own way just as hopelessly imperfect."[1]

The lesson is: Don't be easily distracted by what's next.

4. Can't Recognize It

Because of our fears, opinions, and prejudices, our receptors are too often restricted. You must link your legacy with other people, some very different from you. Contributions that will stand the test of tough times are to be embraced and enjoyed no matter whose idea they were to start with. You will become a much better person when you support others' unique perspectives and celebrate their personal accomplishments.

Always be an encourager, never a labeler.

The lesson is: The number one desire in every heart is to be appreciated.

5. Overpowered

Be careful not to be overly impressed with power and status.

Dorothy was right when she said, "there is no place like home!" Regardless of the price, chef, or service, nothing tastes as good as a home-cooked meal of your favorite foods. Impressive resorts and splendid mansions always lack the comfort of your own pillow and bed back home. Diplomats and generals know the most powerful place on earth is a home filled with faith, hope, and love.

The lesson is: The revolving door of power and the dizzying activities of fame pale to the sweet kiss and welcome hug of a grandchild.

Rock Lesson #11

If you don't know if it's going to be fame or failure, good or bad news, then that's when you really need to focus.

CHAPTER TWELVE

Seven Characteristics of the Rock Solid Life

Tough times make you more appreciative of things sweet and beautiful, important and irreplaceable.

There are seven characteristics in people who have successfully come through tough times:

1. Present – show up consistently, faithfully, completely.

2. Resilient – don't stay down.

3. Attentive – read every word; check every bag.

4. Faithful – no regrets, no reserves, no retreats.

5. Thankful – learn an uplifting prayer and pray it daily.

6. Ready – be prepared, anticipate the unexpected.

7. Humor – Laugh often and especially at yourself.

Here is story of a room full of bright kids who displayed all seven attributes.

Quite the storm suddenly blew into our beautiful little town of Nicholasville, Kentucky. As a matter of fact, we later learned that it was a "drekeo," a straight-line, damaging, and dangerous windstorm. It literally went down the street, knocking out power, breaking out windows, causing severe damage to our high school roof, wailing and hollering as it went.

Mimi was teaching a blended class of third and fourth graders. When the emergency siren went off, she made all the students "assume the position." You know . . . in the hall, sit facing the wall, hands over head—traumatic, to say the least.

After everything quieted, roll call taken, all present, no one hurt, Mimi asked their thoughts of all this commotion.

Four shaken, relieved, and resilient students spoke up.

Monica, a blond haired, deep blue-eyed darling, said, "I gathered the girls around me, and we hugged each other until that storm went away."

"That's good, Monica," Mimi said, "Friends are important."

James, a freckled, red-haired, junior-sized Baptist-preacher-to-be, gathered some friends close around and said, "Boys, it's time to pray."

"That's good, James; faith is very important," Mimi responded.

Michael, destined to be a G.I. Joe for sure, said, "We were brave, very brave, weren't we?"

"For sure!" Mimi said.

Joshua Jedidiah Jones replaced fear with laughter when he said, "I was scared at first. But then after a little while I realized something . . . that no matter what happened today we had a 50-50 chance of seeing . . . Elvis!"

Tough times make you more appreciative of things sweet and beautiful. Each Sunday afternoon, every child at Smootcreek, "if they had behaved," was given a gingerbread cookie and a glass of cold milk. Just like the Dickens story, you didn't dare ask for more. But in the short, crisp, autumn days of fall the life at Smootcreek orphanage (children's home) always took a turn for the better.

Every kid, including my sisters, Caroline and Reva Mae, June Bug, and I marked off the days until the annual Smootcreek pie supper. The stories about the pie supper were told over and over by the older, "I-live here" kids to each new arrival.

At the pie supper it was all-you-can-eat chicken dusted in fresh ground flower and deep fried until golden and crunchy; mounds of mashed potatoes topped with hand-churned, yellow, homemade butter; shucky beans seasoned with real lard and a short slab of salted bacon; lines of ma-son jars filled with pickled beets, bread and butter pickles, pickled eggs, and southern style chow-chow pickled relish; but everyone was warned to stay away from the canned sauerkraut. There were also promises of plates full of soft "light" bread.

Traditions and regimented restrictive behavior yielded their grip this night. Adults stepped back as the kids from Smootcreek were served first. I could scarcely believe it—a chicken breast as big as a hand, the green beans still steaming, we made as big a cavern as possible in our mashed potato mound for the deliciously hard choice of white gravy or brown gravy.

Each family that attended chose Smootcreek children to eat dinner with. I don't recall the family's name that the Mitchell kids ate with that night, just that their daughter was about my age and beautiful. I do remember I managed to eat every bite on my plate.

The old timber-framed school house with its small bell tower was soon filled with foot-stompin' bluegrass music, local front porch players with their banjos, fiddles, basses, and mandolins harmonized, seemingly playing without any effort. Great songs like *Fox on the Run*, *Cripple Creek*, *John Henry*, *Wildwood Flower*, and of course, *Foggy Mountain Breakdown*. The last great classic was to be *I'll fly Away Ole Glory*. But after repeated requests, whistles, and applause they played one more, *I Saw the Light*, because they knew they could get everybody in the place singing and someone would ring the school bell.

With the crowd full, happy, and pleased, the pie auction would begin. Wardy Craft, the Smootcreek director, pointed to the sweet smelling collection of pies that had been eyed and envied all night on a long table covered with a red checkered oil table cloth and a prominently placed sign that read, DO NOT TOUCH!

Wives, to uphold the family's honor, baked dad's favorite fruit pies; deep-dish apple crumb, golden peach with pinched crusts all around, bright red cherry pies with lattice crust generously sprinkled with sugar.

Girlfriends, to impress their suitors, baked cream pies with four-inch high meringue, with the tips of every curl, spike, and swirl browned perfectly.

Widows and the Sunday School Class of the local preacher's wife made sure that there would be enough money raised for the orphan fund by baking several down to earth custard, sweet potato and pumpkin pies.

Soon the cadence of the auctioneer's chant filled the old school with,

"All right now what-ya-give,

"10-10-10 now 15-15-15 now 20."

Then it was on to,

"You-d better not embarrass her,"

"Whose biddin' on your girlfriend's pies?"

"Remember now this is fer them orphans."

Until every pie was sold.

The best moment of the evening came last, as each family shared their costly prize with their Smootcreek kids. In our case, it was the biggest piece of cherry pie that June Bug and I had ever eaten.

To this day my favorite dessert is cherry pie. My first paycheck was earned at Lindsey's Bakery (baker of one of the world's largest pumpkin pies). I still seek out bakeries in every town I visit. I buy gingerbread cookies by the dozen; I like them soft, thick, and with a little sugar cream icing. I love auctions and am a licensed auctioneer. Often I get to shake hands with J.D. Crowe, the legendary bluegrass banjo player. Further proof is the fact that I was fortunate and smart enough to marry the Senior Class Homecoming Queen of Marion College (Indiana Wesleyan University).

Tough times make you more appreciative of things important and irreplaceable. It was some two years before Terry Jacks would pen those hauntingly beautiful lyrics, "Goodbye my friend, it's hard to die" in his hit song, *Seasons in the Sun*, that our family stood by June Bug's hospital bed and listened to strikingly similar words.

All of us tried our best to show courage, but despite four years of hospital rotations, months and months of cobalt radiation, experimental treatments and pain beyond tolerance, at the very end it was June Bug who whispered encouraging words, prayed anointing prayers for his three children, spoke openly of a better place, and extracted promises from each loved one to complete what he could not . . .

Down the list he went . . .

Finish strong.

Only our love for each other lasts forever—not tough times.

Pay attention to life's important stuff: faith, family, friends, God, and country.

Be yourself, but be your *best* self.

Be thankful for the times we had together.

> *We had joy, we had fun*
> *We had Seasons in the Sun*
> *But the hills that we climbed*
> *Were just seasons out of time*

June Bug died from Hodgkin's lymphoma at age 30. He left behind three young precious children. His passing caused me to linger too long in grief's chambers. How could any good come of this?

"*Everybody needs redemptive assistance from outside— from family, friends, ancestors, rules, traditions, institutions, exemplars, and for believers, God.*"[2]

My exemplar was Asbury University Professor Winston Smith. I'll never forget the moment when, ignoring his scheduled biology class, he stopped me at the door, put his hand on my shoulder, and a finger on my problem. I needed help to work through my grief. Forty-five minutes later I had moved from pure misery to precious memories.

To this day, the lesson June Bug taught me—*The Rocks Come with the Farm*—has guided me and inspired me to be a better man.

Rock Lesson #12

Successful people embrace the fact that the rocks come with the farm.

BIBLIOGRAPHY

Chapter 1

1. Bradstreet, Anne. *The Poems of Anne Bradstreet.* Harvard College Library, 1897.

Chapter 2

1. Taleb, Nassim Nicholas. *The Black Swan.* Random House Trade Paperbacks, 2007.
2. Nickell, Patty. *Hilton Head Hurricane.* Lexington Herald-Leader 29 January 2017.
3. Thesaurus.com
4. Murphy, Cait. "The CEO Workout." *Fortune* 10 July 2006: 43-44.
5. *The Holy Bible*, Genesis 50:30
6. Klein, Gerda Weissmann. *All But My Life.* Hill and Wang, 1995.
7. Brooks, David. *The Road to Character.* Random House, 2015.
8. Smith, Wayne B. *Treasures From My Basement.* Wayne B. Smith, 2010.
9. Rendel, Wally

Chapter 3

1. Ades, Kim. *Secret Sauce* and *Frame of Mind Journaling* (Article).
2. McCough, David. *John Adams*

Chapter 4

1. *The Holy Bible*, John 15:13
2. OODA loop, The Free Encyclopedia
3. Payer, S.H. n.d.
4. Harari, Oren. *The Leadership Secrets of Colin Powell*. McGraw-Hill, 2002.
5. Fulghum, Robert. *It Was on Fire When I Lay Down on It*. Villard Books, 1990.

Chapter 6

1. *The Holy Bible*, Psalm 23
2. Thim, Troels, et al. "Initial Assessment and Treatment with the Airway, Breathing, Circulation, Disability, Exposure (ABCDE) Approach." *International Journal of General Medicine* (2012): 117-121.

Chapter 7

1. <www.brainyquote.com/quotes/quotes/r/robertstra128836.html>. Robert Strause

Chapter 8

1. Carlyle, Thomas. <www.brainyquote.com/quotes/quotes/t/thomascarl120878.html>.

2. *Up From Slavery*. Double Day, Page and Co. 1907 (New York, pg. 39).

3. 2016. 29 December 2016. <www.brainyquote. com/quotes/quotes/m/michaeljor127660.html>.

4. Batterson, Mark. *Chase the Lion*. Multnomah, 2016.

5. Klein, Gerta Weissmann. *All But My Life*. Hill and Wang, 1995.

6. Murray, William Hutchinson. *The Scottish Himalayan Expedition*. J.M. Dent & Sons LTD, 1951.

Chapter 9

1. Neibuhr, Reinhold. *Reinhold Neibuhr: Major Works on Religion and Politics*. Ed. Elisabth Sifton. The Library of America, 2015.

2. Maxwell, John C. *Today Matters*

Chapter 10

1. Cicero

2. Armstrong, Louis. "What a Wonderful World." Prod. Bob Thiele. n.d. 30 December 2016. <Genius.com/Louis-Armstrong-what-a-wonderful-world-lyrics.>.

Chapter 12

1. Huxley, Aldous

2. Brooks, David. *The Road to Character*. Random House, 2015.

ABOUT THE AUTHOR

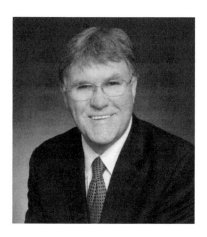

Jonah Mitchell, Ph.D. – Chief Resilience Officer, Realtor, Broker and Developer. An international speaker and teacher. Adjunct Professor at the University of Ken-tucky. Certified instructor for the Kentucky Real Estate Commission. President of Jonah Mitchell Real Estate & Property Management.

Married 47 years to Donna Jean Campbell, father of Jason Mitchell (Dr. Julie Mitchell.) Proud grandfather of Caitlin Jean Mitchell and Aubrey Elizabeth Mitchell.

Jonah is a man of conviction, with a passionate mission to communicate a compelling vision, to maximize innovation, and minimize the impact of the unforeseen.

J onah is an energetic, effective communicator. In the arena of leadership he is a chief resilience officer. He is a man of convictions with a passionate mission to communicate a compelling resilience vision to maximize innovation and minimize the impact of the unforeseen. Jonah will help you and those you influence to develop innovative solutions and strategies to bounce back stronger from life's shocks, stumbles and stresses.

Contact:

Jonah Mitchell, Ph. D

102 Lake St.

Nicholasville, Kentucky 40356

Jonah@jonahmitchell.com

859-887-8870 Office

859-885-8066 Fax

www.therockscomewiththefarm.com